A Funny Thing
Happened on the Way to Church

A Funny Thing Happened on the Way to Church

Compiled by Dave Anderson
Edited by Tim Wilcox

Illustrations by Lance Bowen

Publishing House
St. Louis

MANUFACTURED IN U.S.A.

Library of Congress Cataloging in Publication Data

Main entry under title:

Funny thing happened on the way to church.

1. Clergy—Anecdotes, facetiae, satire, etc.
I. Anderson, David L., 1943-
Timothy J., 1949-
BV663.F86 230 81-311
ISBN0-570-03834-0 AACRI

1 2 3 4 5 6 7 8 9 10 CB 90 89 88 87 86 85 84 83 82 81

Preface

It is hard to imagine a religion of joy without laughter—a gift of God given only to humans. Without mockery, yes, but not without occasional laughter over a foible, a misunderstanding, or an incongruous circumstance.

Even in the church, funny things happen. They serve to break the tension, to puncture pomposity, to dispel gloom, and to restore a sense of proportion when we begin to take ourselves too seriously.

Dave Anderson has collected humorous anecdotes from clergy for some time and felt these were too good to keep to himself. The editing skills of Tim Wilcox present each story succinctly and "in color." We think you'll agree that an eye for the humorous is a trait of the cheerful heart, and—as Solomon wisely noted—"a cheerful heart is a good medicine, but a downcast spirit dries up the bones" (Prov. 17:22).

Dave and Tim herewith say thanks to all contributors, embarrassed and otherwise, who in turn are saying to you, "Here, have a good laugh on us!"

Acknowledgment

Reprinted by permission from the following issues of *The Lutheran:*

THUS SAYS THE PASTOR—June 21, 1978
THAT'S MINISTRY—July 1978
A HIGHER CALLING—Sept. 29, 1978
LADDER-DAY SAINTS—April 18, 1979
CARELESS CONFESSION—Nov. 21, 1979
EQUAL TREATMENT—March 19, 1980
ASNOOZE IN THE PEWS—April 2, 1980
PREACHER PRAISES PRISONERS—April 2, 1980
SIGN UP IN SECRET—May 7, 1980
A TIME FOR MEDICATION—July 1980

Silence, Preacher!

I had been invited to lunch by a family of my congregation. While the mother busied herself in the kitchen, the father and I sat talking in the living room. When the meal was ready, he and I walked slowly to the dining room, talking all the way.

One of the family's young twins, seated at the table and anxious to begin, fixed his eyes on me and interrupted, "Shut up, Rev. Erickson. It's time to eat!"

The parents didn't say a word. Neither did I.

—The Rev. J. E. Erickson
Grover City, Calif.

Don't Look Now, but . . .

Our mission congregation was like a 50-member family. We worshiped in a house that we had converted to a chapel by removing all but two of the walls. In one corner was a small bathroom. The chancel and the seats for the choir were crowded into the space next to it.

One Sunday morning, midway through the organ prelude, a portly soprano hurried out of the little room and crossed in front of the altar to her place in the choir's front row. With her back to the congregation, she leaned over to pick up her hymnal.

A horrified gasp, seeming to come in unison from the 50 worshipers, filled the chapel. Our 190-pound singer had caught the hem of her dress in the top of her girdle. Someone in the choir came to the rescue with a quick hand.

COME BACK HERE
YOU FOOL!
LANCE BOWEN

Meanwhile, members of the congregation were leafing diligently through their hymnals, searching for the processional hymn. Standing in back, I could hardly wait for the first stanza.

—The Rev. Paul O. Hamsher
Williamsburg, Va.

Come Back Here!

When our veteran church organist went away to college, one of the replacements was her younger sister, who had just begun taking organ lessons. I hadn't noticed how regularly our previous organist would leave the organ loft when the sermon began, taking the back stairs to the basement and returning just before the sermon ended. So I paid little attention to the fact that our fledgling organist had picked up her sister's habit. Until . . .

It was during one of our Lenten vesper services. I got into the pulpit and began my sermon with what I thought was a gripping illustration:

> At the height of one of the battles of the Civil War, a young soldier thought he heard the command to charge. Leaping out of the trench with the regimental flag, he started running across no-man's-land toward the blazing fire of the enemy line. When his captain saw that other soldiers were running out of the trenches to follow the flag bearer, he shouted at the top of his voice [as I did that evening]: "Come back here, you fool!"

Immediately, I heard the clatter of footsteps in the back of the church as our young organist emerged breathless to take her place on the organ bench. She never left the organ loft again during a sermon.

—The Rev. Jaroslav J. Vajda
St. Louis, Mo.

Shameless Shepherds

During a special Christmas service for children, Sunday school students were asked questions about the birth of Jesus. In response to "What did the shepherds find when they came to Bethlehem?" an excited eight-year-old raised her hand. "I know," she said. "They found Mary and Joseph lying in the manger."

—The Rev. G. M. Krach
Saginaw, Mich.

A Father's Children

Several blocks from the Lutheran church where I served as pastor was a Roman Catholic elementary school.

One morning after making calls in the neighborhood, I came upon two boys walking home from the school. I recognized one of them. The other, whom I didn't know, saw my clerical collar and said brightly, "Good morning, Father."

His companion gasped and jabbed him in the ribs. "He ain't no father," said the lad I knew. "He's got kids!"

—The Rev. William Nolting
Stratford, Ont., Canada

Pardon Me, Um . . .

The groom was Lutheran, a member of my congregation; the bride, Roman Catholic. At the postwedding reception dinner, one of the waiters, evidently Catholic, came by with a tray of drinks.

"HE AIN'T NO FATHER! HE'S GOT KIDS!"
ZAPMAN
LANCE BOWEN

"Will you have one, Father?" he asked me. Then he noticed my wife, seated next to me. "Uh, pardon me, how about you—um, uh—Mrs. Father?"

—The Rev. William Nolting
Stratford, Ont., Canada

Lest Ye Fall Asleep

I was preaching one Sunday morning on the passage in Mark 10 about blind Bartimaeus. The account of Jesus' healing miracle is full of drama, and I wanted to convey it to the congregation. Speaking quietly at first, I built up to the moment when Bartimaeus cries out, "Jesus, Son of David, have mercy on me!"

I cried out. Immediately to my right was the choir. One of the tenors, who had been sleeping peacefully, leaped to his feet, eyes bugging out.

Bartimaeus was forgotten as everyone stared at the startled tenor. I paused, half expecting him to say something like, "I don't know what we're voting for, Pastor, but you and I are the only ones in favor of it."

So much for my dramatic sermon.

—The Rev. Marvin Rygh
Redondo Beach, Calif.

Such a Reputation!

Although I was retired, a young man came to our home to make arrangements for his wedding.

"Will you marry us in the town-square park, Pastor?" he asked.

I told him the park usually was full of tourists. There would be no privacy.

Then he looked through the living room window and saw our oleander bush in full bloom. "Will you marry us there?"

I hesitated but was won over by his enthusiasm for our bush. The couple was married not long after in our yard, almost encircled by the oleander.

A few weeks later, I picked up the phone and listened as someone with a girlish voice asked hopefully, "Is this the minister who marries people under the bushes?"

What could I say?

—The Rev. Niels Nielsen
Solvang, Calif.

Luther Was a Pest

The young church in Guyana, South America, had just begun to hold national conventions. At one of these early gatherings, a speaker lectured about the Reformation.

Listening intently, one of the delegates, who was from a remote parish on the Berbice River, heard the word *theses* again and again. He remembered it and, returning home, offered this summary to his congregation:

"Martin Luther *teased* the pope once. He teased him twice and three times. He kept on teasing the pope until he teased him 95 times. Well, the pope couldn't bear this any longer, so he fired Luther, who went away and started his own church."

—The Rev. Hector C. Magalee
Rainbow Lakes, N.J.

Don't Blame Her, Please!

It happened 50 years ago in Wisconsin. The custom in my friend's church at that time was for fathers to register themselves and their family members for Communion. To do this they would meet the pastor in the sacristy before the service.

One Sunday morning a farmer hurried into that room just as the organist was finishing her prelude. His arm, broken or sprained, was in a sling.

Worried about being late and startled by the farmer's injury, the pastor momentarily forgot his parishioner's name; so he asked, "You and Mrs. uh . . .?"

"Oh, no!" protested the farmer. "It was the horse. He kicked me."

—The Rev. N. W. Stoa
Seattle, Wash.

What's in a Name?

A common practice among families living on the Berbice River in Guyana, South America, was to name their children after famous people, past and present. You could walk into the villages and meet Augustine, Shakespeare, Rockefeller, and others.

During one Baptism service, the pastor asked the sponsor what name had been chosen for the child. "Pin-pan-he," answered the sponsor. But the pastor didn't understand and asked again. "Pin-pan-he," came the reply, this time with urgency. So the infant was baptized "Pin-pan-he."

Filling in the baptismal certificate after the service, the pastor asked about the spelling of "Pin-pan-he."

"IT WAS THE HORSE! HE KICKED ME!"
LANCE BOWEN

Only then did he discover that the sponsor had been trying to tell him that the name was *pinned* on the child's pants. The real name, carefully recorded on the certificate: "Montgomery Ward."

—The Rev. Hector C. Magalee
Rainbow Lakes, N.J.

Marital or Martial?

A Presbyterian pastor-colleague of mine, whom I came to know in Wenatchee, Wash., told me about a wedding he performed for a young soldier and his bride.

At that time—shortly after World War II—the nuptial kiss in the Presbyterian wedding service followed the minister's instruction "You may salute the bride."

Upon hearing these words, the soldier first looked astonished. But trained to regard an order as an order, he executed a left turn, performed a snappy salute to his beloved, then turned sharply right, and stood at attention, waiting for the service to proceed.

—The Rev. John M. Eggen
Martinsburg, W. Va.

Cordial Canines

They were older, probably in their 60s, and they wanted to be married. Marvelous, I thought. So we sat down in my office to get acquainted and to discuss plans for the wedding.

I soon discovered that one of the things that had brought them together was their passion for dogs. On and on they went about their three pets. But I didn't realize how important these companions were until the couple showed me the proposed wording for their wedding invitation. It began, "Fred, Angel, and Twinkle request the honor of your presence at the marriage of their owners. . . ."

—The Rev. Clemens Pera
Seattle, Wash.

Farewell, Dear Pastor

Some years ago, a pastor in North Dakota told me about an "end times" experience at the parish he had served for many years. For some reason most of the congregation disliked him. They were anxious for their shepherd to leave.

Finally, a call came. Sunday morning he announced his decision to accept the call. Spontaneously, the entire congregation arose and sang with gusto, "Praise God from Whom All Blessings Flow."

—Bishop E. O. Gilbertson
Sioux Falls, S. Dak.

A Eunuch Approach

As a student at Luther Theological Seminary, St. Paul, Minn., in the early 1930s, I sang in the male chorus. During our concerts at the churches we visited, one of us would lead in Scripture reading and prayer. Most of the devotionals were forgettable, but one remains in my memory as a "highlight" of those years.

A second-year student had selected the passage

from Acts 8 that tells about Philip's conversion of the Ethiopian eunuch. After reading the account, he paused for a moment. Then, in a tone of great spiritual concern, he looked out over the congregation and said, "I'm sure there are many eunuchs here tonight."

What he said after that, including his prayer, I don't recall. I do remember that we barely stifled our laughter and, after the service, roasted him all the way back to the seminary.

—The Rev. N. W. Stoa
Seattle, Wash.

Bird of Promise

The funniest incident of my 40-year ministry took place in the parsonage living room during a wedding. Immediately after the bride and groom had said "I do," our clock sounded the hour: "Cuckoo, cuckoo, cuckoo"!

—The Rev. Luther Miles Schulze
Baltimore, Md.

Chicken à la Funk

Pastor and Mrs. John August Johns of Funk, Nebr., were sleeping peacefully one night. Suddenly, Mrs. Johns was awakened by a noise that seemed to come from the chicken house; so she woke her husband, who went outside to check.

Approaching the chicken house, he saw a young man holding a gunny sack half full of clucking chickens. The youth spotted him, dropped the sack, and ran.

CUCKOO
CUCKOO
CUCKOO
LANCE

Without saying a word, Pastor Johns picked up the sack. Chickens kept coming until someone inside asked, "How many do we have now?" In his best preacher's voice, the parson replied, "Five—since I started holding the sack."

—The Rev. Roger Ose
Minneapolis, Minn.

A Dubious Compliment

Reformation Sunday 1966. The service was over, and Pastor Al Storvik of Lakewood, Calif., stood at the church door greeting worshipers.

One woman, smiling brightly, grasped his hand and chirped, "Oh, thank you, Pastor, for your sermon. I've always liked that one!"

—The Rev. Les Hoffmann
Phoenix, Ariz.

Pipe Down, or Else!

For several years I was pastor of two parishes in rural Portland, N. Dak. Although small, these churches had public address systems, mainly for the hard of hearing. Volume controls were mounted on the pulpit where I could reach them.

Sunday morning in one of the churches, the children seemed unusually restless. So, hoping to put the adults at ease, I simply announced, "Mothers, if your children are too noisy, don't worry. I have a button up here to take care of it." On with the sermon.

A couple of days later, one of my parishioners

suggested that I rephrase my "button announcement." A family that rented from her had been guests in church that Sunday. Their eight-year-old daughter, normally an uncontrollable bundle of energy, had sat through most of the service like a rock. Worried, her mother had asked, "What's the matter, honey? Are you sick?"

In a whisper, the little girl had answered, "No, Mommy, but what'll happen if he pushes that button?"

—The Rev. William Breen
Pulaski, Wis.

Sin Boldly

The seminary student obviously was nervous as he led Sunday morning worship. After the invocation, he turned to face the congregation and said, "Let us now transgress our confessions."

—The Rev. Bob Kasperson
Chicago, Ill.

Let Us Pray the Creed

While in Wisconsin serving my first parish, I was asked to take part in the installation service of a neighboring congregation's new pastor. On the way to the church I began to feel foggy-headed. "I'm coming down with something," I said to my wife, "but I'll make it through the service."

I did—sort of . . . One of my responsibilities was to lead the confession of faith. Wobbling out to chancel center, I said, "Now let us confess our faith in the words of the Apostles' Creed: Our Father, who art in heaven . . . ," I began, and everyone followed.

Halfway through, however, one of the pastors standing off to one side decided to correct my error. "I believe in the Holy Ghost; the holy Christian church, the Communion . . . ," he boomed out, and everyone followed him.

After "the Life everlasting," I stumbled back to my chair, wondering who was more confused—me or the congregation.

—The Rev. Alvin Pinke
Bakersfield, Calif.

Your Chances Are 50/50

Years ago in Wisconsin, a pastor friend of mine complimented a young couple on their beautiful little boy.

"She's a girl!" said the mother. "You ought to know, Pastor. You baptized her two weeks ago."

Flustered, my friend smiled awkwardly and replied, "Yes, yes, of course. Well, I knew it was one or the other."

—The Rev. N. W. Stoa
Seattle, Wash.

Guess Who's Really in Charge

I'll never forget the time I was teaching members of a confirmation class about the Ten Commandments. During one session, we focused on the Sixth Commandment, "Thou shalt not commit adultery."

At the beginning of class, I asked if anyone could find the Bible verse that says a man should only have one wife. A hand shot up. "Well, Pastor," volunteered one of my brighter students, "isn't it the verse that says no man can serve two masters?"

—The Rev. Les Hoffmann
Phoenix, Ariz.

Preacher's Promotion

I had to be away from my church one Sunday. When the visiting pastor stepped into the pulpit, a little girl in the congregation looked up and loudly inquired, "Mommy, where is God this morning?"

—The Rev. Wilbur E. Allen
Seal Beach, Calif.

For Better, for Worse

This is about a wedding. I was one of the guests, not the officiating minister. Thank goodness!

Anyway, it was a hot and humid day. Shortly after the wedding party arrived at the altar, the best man fainted. Reviving on the floor, he whispered to the groom, "I forgot the rings." The groom passed the word to one of the groomsmen, who went off to get a glass of water. On his way back, he stopped among the guests to get his wife's ring and then took off his own. But before he could hand the rings over, the groom fainted.

About that time the minister said, "How about bringing some chairs up for these people." So they all sat down for the marriage homily.

The pastor looked fine, but his first line, addressed to Peter, the groom, was "Peter, Peter, pumpkin eater, had a wife and couldn't keep her." Next he turned to Mary, the bride, "Mary, Mary, quite contrary."

Then, to emphasize the problems that can arise in marriage, he recited, "Jack Spratt could eat no fat, his wife could eat no lean."

This was just too much for the bride's mother, who thudded on the front pew in a dead faint.

Other than that, the ceremony went off without incident.

—The Rev. Clarence W. Stradtman
Elkhorn, Wis.

Reading from the, Uh . . . Woops

It was time for the Epistle Lesson. The pastor stepped up to the lectern and began to read. Several verses later he realized it was not the appointed text for that Sunday. So he read a few more lines, then solemnly concluded with "Here ends the wrong Epistle."

—Bishop E. O. Gilbertson
Sioux Falls, S. Dak.

Laundered Loot

A clergy colleague of mine, Pastor J. J., told me about a mental lapse he had one Sunday morning. The offering had been collected and the ushers came forward.

After the singing of the offertory, he stepped toward the altar, plates in hand. But to everyone's astonishment, Pastor J. J. passed the altar and headed directly for the chancel corner, where he carefully dumped envelopes, bills, and coins into the baptismal font.

"I don't know what came over me," he said.

My guess is that, subconsciously, he believes in holy water, and that he was trying to cleanse that filthy lucre.

—The Rev. Alvin Pinke
Bakersfield, Calif.

Let Him Who Boasts . . .

While I was traveling with a Gospel team several years ago, I preached in a Wisconsin congregation. At the church door afterwards, a Scandinavian saint grabbed my hand and exclaimed, "My, that was wonderful!"

I thanked him and humbly replied, "It was just Jesus."

"No," said he, "it wasn't that good."

—Cliff Peterson
Huntington Beach, Calif.

The Rev. I. M. N. Outhouse

I was shaking hands at the church door after preaching a dynamite sermon on how John the Baptist prepared the way for the Messiah. Up stepped my favorite parishioner, beaming as usual. "Pastor," she said, "you're my John."

—The Rev. Arley Fadness
Harrisburg, S. Dak.

What Can He Possibly Mean?

Let's call him "Dr. L." As a visiting dignitary and one of the keynote speakers at a church women's convention, he maintained a high profile throughout the event.

After Dr. L's first speech, the chairwoman announced procedures for the noon meal. "Ladies," she said, "because there are too many of us to serve at one sitting, we'll eat in two shifts."

The honorable Dr. L, of course, was invited to eat with the first group. On his way out of the dining hall after lunch, he noticed a line of women standing near a door by the entry way. Smiling broadly and remembering the tasty food, he waved to them and shouted, "Ladies, I can tell you that it's well worth waiting for!"

Instead of smiles in response to his friendly remark, Dr. L noted a lineup of bewildered faces. Then he saw it—on the door, in large black letters: WOMEN.

—The Rev. Ed Hansen
New Hope, Minn.

Deliver Her from This Affliction

Back in the early 1950s, I was a freshman at Augustana Academy in Sioux Falls, S. Dak. In those days it was the custom for academy students to spend part of Sunday afternoon at a nearby hospital. Going from room to room in small delegations, we would visit the sick and take turns praying for their recovery.

On one of my first afternoons at the hospital, I dreaded having to pray. Room after room went by, and I wasn't called on. When we came to the last patient on our list, I heard, "Arley, will you pray?"

..."IT'S WELL WORTH WAITING FOR!"
WOMEN
LANCE BOWEN

My relief evaporated. To my surprise, though, I came up with an eloquent prayer, asking God to heal this woman and spare her any recurrence of the illness. "Amen!" I finished, with conviction.

In the hall afterwards, I was puzzled by our adviser's broad smile and my classmates' barely suppressed laughter. What had I done?

Then they told me: We were in the maternity ward!

—The Rev. Arley Fadness
Harrisburg, S. Dak.

What to Do?

"I almost decided to leave the ministry," said a young pastor after the first funeral in his first church. Why?

The family of the deceased was poor and could only afford a pine-box coffin. After the service, as the pallbearers were leaving the church, the coffin bottom broke loose. Out rolled the corpse, down the steps. The mourners screamed, and the pastor froze.

Surely the funeral director will know what to do, he thought. But no. Lying on the ground, not far from the corpse, was the undertaker—in a dead faint.

—The Rev. Leland Bottjen
Spokane, Wash.

A Talented Sinner

A few years ago I went back to Glenam, S. Dak., for anniversary celebrations of the Norwegian Lutheran congregation there. I was to sing a solo during the

Communion service. Imagine my chagrin when I opened the bulletin on Sunday morning. There I read that "Pastor Ray Peterson will be *sinning* during the distribution."

—The Rev. Ray Peterson
Sioux Falls, S. Dak.

Telltale Tombstone

A man who had lost his wife came to me for counseling. During our several sessions, the phrase he used most often was "I loved her so much that I'll never marry again."

Several months later he came to me and said, "Pastor, I have a real problem. I've met another woman."

"What's the matter with that?" I asked.

His answer: "I said I'd never marry again. Worse than that, I had 'My light has gone out' inscribed on my wife's tombstone."

"No problem," I said, after thinking for a minute. "Just inscribe this underneath it: 'I have struck another match.'"

—The Rev. Les Hoffmann
Phoenix, Ariz.

Nothing Refreshes Like . . .

A pastor friend of mine had an alcoholic come to him for counseling. During one of their sessions, the man asked for Holy Communion.

Better not use the wine, my friend thought. So he

called the janitor and asked him to get some Welch's grape juice at a nearby store.

Almost an hour later, the janitor returned. "Get everything ready for communion," said the pastor. A few minutes later he turned to the alcoholic and said, "Let's go into the church, and may the Lord's Supper strengthen you." So they did. Afterward, the alcoholic shook the pastor's hand vigorously, professing to be greatly refreshed.

On the way back to his office, my friend stopped to thank the janitor for his help. "You're welcome, Pastor," said the janitor, "But I did have a little problem at the store."

"What was that?" asked the pastor.

"Well," replied the janitor, "not only were they out of Welch's, but they didn't have any grape juice at all. So, after thinking a while, I got the next best thing—Dad's Old-Fashioned Root Beer."

—The Rev. Alvin Pinke
Bakersfield, Calif.

Hot-Air Confession

At one time St. Lorenz Church in Frankenmuth, Mich., had an organ whose "wind" was supplied by a manual pump. Two people were needed to play the instrument: an organist and a pumper.

On one occasion, when a visiting preacher was leading worship, the organist sensed that her instrument was running out of wind at a crucial point in the service. Leading the Creed, the substitute pastor was going much more slowly than the regular pastor.

"Mere Wind [more wind]!" hissed the organist to the pumper.

In an offended tone of voice, the pumper fairly boomed over the organ notes, *"Ich weiss doch wieviel Wind der Glaube nimmt* [I think I know how much wind the confession takes]!"

—The Rev. Paul F. Hartmann
Dwight, Ill.

Naughty Pastor

The image of ministerial other-worldliness is deeply rooted in the minds of many people. That certainly was true of a 16-year-old girl in our first parish.

When news of my wife's first pregnancy reached the girl's mother, she shared it with her daughter. "Isn't it wonderful?" said the mother. "The pastor's wife is expecting."

The girl weighed the news for a long time and finally said, "Yes—but Reverend . . . but Reverend . . . ?!"

—The Rev. Jaroslav Vajda
St. Louis, Mo.

A Novice's Oversight

My first wedding was at Bethel Lutheran Church in Madison, Wis. As I stood up front awaiting the wedding party, I suddenly realized that no one had mentioned special music. "A novice's oversight," I said to myself, "but it'll be OK."

It wasn't. After the bride, groom, and attendants had arrived at the altar, a soloist appeared several feet away, next to the organist. Clad in an extremely low-cut formal gown, she began crooning, in night-club style, "Tonight We Love."

—The Rev. Reuben Gornitzka
Edina, Minn.

You're Not Smiling, Grandpa

Years ago in southern Minnesota, it was the custom for Lutheran pastors to have services in the homes of bereaved parishioners before the church funeral. Often, the body remained at home for viewing by family members.

On one occasion the local pastor went out to a farm for such a service. When he arrived, he found family members and relatives posing together for the town photographer. Nothing surprising about that.

Stepping up to the group with a word of comfort on his lips, the pastor suddenly stopped in his tracks. Smiling in unison, family members were gathered around grandpa, who was leaning against a tree—in his casket!

—The Rev. Bob Kasperson
Chicago, Ill.

Beginner's Luck

It was the first hospital call of my ministry, and I wanted it to go well. Dos and don'ts firmly in mind, I walked anxiously to the patient's room. There she was—a woman in her 80s who, the nurses had told me, was senile.

Just as I was about to intone a carefully practiced

LANCE BOWEN

greeting, she leaped up on the bed with surprising agility—and without a stitch of clothing.

My composure all but gone, I garbled, "Ma'am, can I help you with something?

"Gotta go to the bathroom, gotta go the the bathroom," she squeaked.

Well, one thing I knew was that my job as a pastor was to minister to spiritual needs, and this obviously was a physical need. So I rushed into the hallway, looking for a nurse or an orderly. Nobody in sight. What to do?

I went back to the room and she was still standing there—an impatient patient. Completely befuddled by now, I could only manage, "Ma'am, there's nobody out there, but I'll be back next week."

Before I could escape, she fairly screamed at me, "Young man, I can't wait till next week to go to the bathroom!"

—The Rev. Wally Klandrud
Phoenix, Ariz.

Don't Forget Her What!

Two people came to me and said, "We want to be married." The groom-to-be was 81; his bride, only a youngster, was 76.

I agreed (they were in love) and, a few weeks later, found myself standing in front of a small group of their closest friends. The ceremony went smoothly until the exchange of rings.

"I can't get it on," broadcast the groom, straining to overcome his bride's knuckle barrier.

The best man, who was older than the groom, fairly shouted, "Spit on it!" That worked.

After the ceremony was over and the couple was making their honeymoon exit, the matron of honor called after the bride, "Do you have your pills?"

She meant the bride's blood-pressure pills, but the guests were laughing too hard to hear the explanation.

—The Rev. Homer Larsen
Cedar Falls, Iowa

Equal Treatment

As a campus pastor I encourage lectors at our services to use inclusive language as a way of witnessing to the wholeness of both male and female in God's creation.

Chuckles erupted, however, when one young woman amended a portion of the Second Lesson, Galatians 5:1-15, in this way: "Now I, Paul, say to you that if you receive circumcision, Christ will be of no advantage. I testify again to every person, man or woman, who receives circumcision that that person is bound to keep the whole law."

—The Rev. Darlene E. Grega
Durham, N. C.

Reflections in a Small Room

Years ago in Burnaby, B.C., Canada, I was asked to conduct the funeral of a young man who had left behind a wife and several children. As there was no opportunity to visit the widow prior to the day of the funeral, I arranged to meet with her before the service.

At the funeral chapel, I was ushered into a room

reserved for the bereaved. For 15 minutes I listened to the tragic story of how this woman's husband had been killed in a logging accident. We had a brief prayer and, rising to negotiate the maze of doors and corridors leading to the sanctuary, I said, "I'll be thinking of you when I'm in there."

Of course, I meant the chapel. But a moment later, after stepping through a door, I found myself in the bathroom. Red-faced, I opened the door, marched through the room for the bereaved, and struggled to regain my composure for the funeral liturgy.

—The Rev. Lee Luetkehoelter
Winnipeg, Man., Canada

Half-Time Entertainment

In the church of my boyhood, it was the custom to have a solo during the offering. When the singer was finished, the ushers would march forward to the chancel. Because of the high-church emphasis in this congregation, timing was important.

One Sunday morning the collection plates were passed with clockwork efficiency to the strains of a beautiful soprano solo. After two or three verses there was an organ interlude, which the ushers took to be the signal for coming forward. Marching in step, they were halfway up the center aisle when the soloist started another verse.

What followed was a marvel of drill-team precision. Without a word, the four stopped simultaneously in their tracks, did an about-face, and marched back to the narthex.

—The Rev. Les Hoffmann
Phoenix, Ariz.

A Grave Mistake

At the burial service for a military man, taps were blown and a volley was fired. The rifle shots were too much for one elderly woman, who fell on the grass in a dead faint.

Anger flaring in his eyes, the woman's nine-year-old grandson raced to her side, then shouted at the top of his voice, "The sons of ------- shot Grandma!"

—The Rev. H. W. Niermann
Cheyenne, Wyo.

What *Do* You Call Him?

Some pastors' first names are unusual, but few are as strange as mine.

Several weeks after we had arrived at our first parish, members of the congregation were beginning to feel comfortable with us—comfortable enough for one of the women to ask my wife, "Just what *do* you call your husband?"

Without hestiation, she replied, "Your Holiness."

—The Rev. Jaroslav Vajda
St. Louis, Mo.

I Will Make You Fishers . . .

For several weeks the pastor had ignored pleas for counseling from a parishioner who simply wanted to take his time—by the hours.

Now this was a large church with a wrap-around balcony, one end of which loomed over the pulpit. The sanctuary was full one Sunday morning—about 2,000

LANCE

worshipers—when the pastor stepped into the pulpit to preach. A few lines into his sermon, he was startled into silence by a piece of paper floating down from the balcony. He looked up and, sure enough, there was the disgruntled parishioner, slowing paying out line from a fishing rod he was holding over the railing.

Regaining his composure, the pastor unhooked the note, excused himself, met with the man to make an appointment, then returned to finish the sermon.

—The Rev. Ray Lindquist
Hollywood, Calif.

To the Rescue

Mary and Bill were about to be married. Before the ceremony I sensed that Mary might not make it. Bill didn't look too rugged either, so I gave an ammonia capsule to the bride's father—just in case someone fainted.

Let's get 'em married, I thought. Everything went just fine until the couple knelt for their wedding prayer. After "Amen," Mary didn't get up. In fact, she was pretty much lying down on the kneeling pad.

Coolly, I gave a nod to her father, who rushed up to the rail with a confused look on his face. As I knelt to raise Mary for the ammonia treatment, he broke the capsule and held it under *my* nose. Poof! The top of my head went off as Mary slept on peacefully.

"What should I do?" asked her father.

Fading quickly, all I could think of was "Carry her out!"

The benediction was never pronounced.

—The Rev. Homer Larsen
Cedar Falls, Iowa

Never on Sunday

Every now and then "shirttail relatives" of the church call on the clergy to perform weddings. Often, these "strangers" know little about the faith and its traditions.

This was true of the folks who asked me to perform a home ceremony. Reluctantly, I agreed.

On the way there I worried that things would get out of hand. When I arrived things were out of hand. The punch bowl was full of some sort of powerful brew and everybody was enjoying it. Better get this thing under way, I thought.

We did. The bride and groom stood on one side of the punch bowl. I stood on the other and began the solemn ceremony: "Dear friends in Christ, we are—"

All of a sudden, the bride cried out, "Oh, my! Oh, my! The music!"

How nice, I thought, marking my place. Someone ran to the record player and dropped the needle. When the music boomed from the speakers, my worst fears were realized.

To the tune of "Never on Sunday," over a punch bowl full of booze, I got those two married. Mercy!

—The Rev. Wally Klandrud
Phoenix, Ariz.

A Chicken's Way Out

In my first parish—a rural congregation—I rattled around in the parsonage unmarried for 15 months. Fortunately, I was blessed with wonderful members and neighbors who frequently invited me over for dinner.

I recall one meal in particular. The invitation came during the second day of a heavy storm. Said my parishioner: "One of our chickens stayed out in the rain and drowned. Why don't you come over and help us eat it?"

I thought she was kidding, but at the table her husband recounted the tragedy: "It was the funniest thing. Yesterday, when it was raining hardest, this fool chicken stood outdoors, looking skyward with its mouth open. Suddenly, it dropped over, fluttered a bit, then lay still. I took it to the hen house but it was too late. So here you are, Pastor, helping us eat a bird that committed suicide."

Farewell, appetite!

—The Rev. F. W. Hofmann
Pottstown, Pa.

Let Me Rephrase That

A pastor in a small Midwestern city was noted for his faithful hospital visits. He would take time for people whether or not they were members of his church.

One woman who had been ill for several weeks and who was not a parish member came to church soon after her release from the hospital. She wanted to thank the pastor for his concern and to hear him preach. After the service she stood in line to shake his hand. Behind her was one of the congregation's most solemn and conservative deacons.

At the door the woman realized that the pastor didn't recognize her. "Remember me?" she asked. "You've been calling on me at the hospital for the past several weeks."

"YOU'D CRY TOO."....
LANCE BOWEN

"Oh, yes!" replied the pastor. "I've just never seen you with your clothes on before."

—Bishop E. O. Gilbertson
Sioux Falls, S. Dak.

Enough to Make You Weep

As a seminary student, I was sent one Sunday to preach at a suburban congregation. Following the service, a family invited me to their home for a chicken dinner. It was good!

After dinner the hostess asked if I'd like to walk in the garden with Leroy, her six-year-old son. Outdoors, Leroy and I came upon a group of little chicks peeping forlornly.

"They seem to be crying," I said to Leroy.

"Well," he replied, "you'd cry too if someone just ate your mama."

—The Rev. F. W. Hofmann
Pottstown, Pa.

Ungrateful Snob!

It was my birthday. At the ladies' guild meeting, I opened with devotions. After "Amen," they surprised me with a golf bag full of clubs and a rousing rendition of "Happy Birthday."

I was speechless. But, being a pastor, I *had* to say something and offered a few words of thanks. Then they surprised me again—this time with a chorus of laughter.

Completely befuddled, I asked, "Why are you

laughing? All I said was 'I'm sure I don't deserve this, but I really do appreciate it.' "

"Pastor," said the chairwoman, "that might have been what you had in your heart, but what we heard was 'I'm sure I don't appreciate this, but I really do deserve it.' "

—The Rev. L. W. Schuth
Joliet, Ill.

Such a Welcome!

The Sunday service included the installation of a new teacher, who had been ushered to a special chair in front of the congregation. After the organ prelude, everyone began singing the first hymn. Startled, the pastor realized it was not the one he had chosen. So he quickly summoned an elder of the congregation. "What is this hymn we are singing?" asked the pastor.

"Oh," replied the elder, "it's one from the 'Cross and Affliction' section."

The hymn, erroneously posted, was No. 352 in the German Lutheran hymnal: *"Ach Gott, wie manches Herzeleid begegnet mir zu dieser Zeit!"* Freely translated, the words mean "O God, what a terrible grief has befallen us at this time!"

—The Rev. E. M. Goltermann
Milwaukee, Wis.

The Father's What!

When I was serving a Lutheran congregation in Davenport, Iowa, my wife often would get phone calls for "the father." She would tell the callers that they wanted Holy Family *Catholic* Church, not Holy Cross *Lutheran* Church.

One day an elderly woman called and asked to speak with the father. My wife explained the mistake. Well, this woman called again. Once more my wife patiently explained, "You want Holy Family. . . ." The phone rang a third time and, sure enough, it was the same woman.

"By the way," she asked, "who am I speaking to?" The answer: "You are speaking to the father's *wife!*"

Bang went the receiver. Message received!

—The Rev. Walter S. Wendt
Davenport, Iowa

When the Pastor's Away, the People . . .

The pastor of a small congregation in a western state had to be absent one Sunday during Advent because of a conference. Rather than ask another pastor to preach, the people decided to stage a *Lese-gottesdienst,* or reading service. One of the elders volunteered to read a sermon. Another said, "I'll play the organ."

Sunday came. There was no prelude, and the congregation soon discovered why. The elder at the keyboard started playing the opening hymn, "O How Shall I Receive Thee?"—with one finger.

"Oh how shall . . . O how . . . O . . . O," they began. Soon some were singing "O . . . O" and some "how . . . how," while others simply hummed bars of the hymn at random.

After a few minutes of this chaos, one of the leaders stood up and shouted, "I move that we pray the Lord's Prayer and go home." Which they did.

—The Rev. Samuel E. Rathke
Evanston, Ill.

Step into My Office

From the comfortable distance of four decades, pastor J. K. can bring himself to recall the trauma of something that happened during his early ministry in the Virginia farmlands.

The rambling parsonage, the white frame church, and the parish cemetery formed an island that was at least a mile from the nearest neighbor. One muggy Saturday evening the pastor decided it was safe to take his bath in the back yard of the parsonage. Relaxing in a washtub, he was startled out of his reverie by the sudden appearance of headlights around the corner of the house.

There he was—stranded. And there was nothing to do but deal with the unexpected parishioner's problem, mustering all the dignity he could in that most unlikely office.

—The Rev. Jaroslav Vajda
St. Louis, Mo.

But I Love Him!

A pastor I knew told me about a pastor he knew who was conducting a wedding service. During the exchange of vows, he said, "Now, dear bride, do you

LANCE
BOWEN

take . . ." Suddenly the pages in his service book flipped over. Struggling to find his place again, the pastor inadvertently turned to the baptismal service.

Addressing the bride and glancing at the groom, he intoned, "Dear bride, uh, do you renounce this devil, and all his works, and all his ways?"

—Bishop E. O. Gilbertson
Sioux Falls, S. Dak.

Twice As Much Fun

Years ago in Nebraska it was the law that a couple obtain their marriage license in the county where they were to be married. Whether or not that requirement is still on the books, I don't know.

I do know that I wish it hadn't been for one particular wedding. The day before the ceremony the bride came to town from Lincoln, 50 miles away, where she was a college student. I had asked her to bring the license to the rehearsal, but she forgot. "Don't worry," I said. "We'll take care of it tomorrow."

Tomorrow came. So did a lot of people—to the wedding. We breezed through the ceremony without a hitch and then joined in a fancy reception. Midway through the cake and coffee I invited the witnesses into my office to sign the marriage license. They did. As I was scrawling my own name, though, I noticed a line of not-so-small print: "Valid in Lancaster County only." Help! We were in Douglas County, and I had just performed an invalid wedding.

Quickly I found the bride's father and said, "Please make sure the couple doesn't leave until I've solved a minor problem." Back in my office, I called a lawyer.

His advice: "Drive over to Lancaster County, across the line, and marry them again."

A nuisance, but what else could we do? So I rounded up the bride, groom, maid of honor, and best man. We hopped in a car and headed down Interstate 80, eyes peeled for a sign that read "Entering Lancaster County."

Thirty-five miles later we saw it and pulled off the road immediately. Right there—on a patch of weed-strewn gravel, with cars, buses, and trucks honking as they passed—I married those two again.

Accounts of that "double wedding" were in the papers the next day. But the bride and groom missed the headlines. They weren't about to wait around for a third attempt.

—The Rev. Paul Ruff
Brandenton, Fla.

His Name, You Fool!

A sailor and his fiancée asked a navy chaplain to perform their wedding. Several hours before the ceremony, the chaplain said a few words about the marriage service to the couple, but he didn't go into detail. "You'll get your cues from me," he told them.

When it was time for the real thing, the bride seemed perfectly calm. Her husband-to-be, however, looked pale and nervous. But he performed well until the exchange of rings.

"Repeat after me," said the chaplain to the groom, "With this ring I thee wed." The sailor managed that line. Next the chaplain intoned, "In the name of the Father." Nothing from the groom. "Uh, um . . . In the

LANCE

name of the Father," said the chaplain again. More silence. Once more he spoke to the sailor, this time with fading patience, *"In the name of the Father."*

Despairing, the groom croaked, "But I don't know her father's name!"

—The Rev. Les Hoffmann
Phoenix, Ariz.

Tell Me I'm Dreaming

I was sitting at home one Saturday afternoon, daydreaming. All of a sudden I remembered: wedding, 3 p.m. It was almost three!

No time to change. I hopped in my car and sped to church. Once there, I peeked through a side door and saw, much to my horror, the wedding attendants at the altar.

Mad dash to my office. No keys! Out to the car, then back. Halfway across the church lawn, the automatic sprinklers went on. In the sacristy, I frantically donned my surplice and then tripped out into the chancel area.

Members of the wedding party smiled broadly—but not because they were happy to see me. I was soaking wet!

—The Rev. Bill Vaswig
Issaquah, Wash.

Careless Confession

While preaching at a Lutheran nursing home in the Minneapolis area, a pastor waved his arms toward the congregation, saying, "You have sinned!" Then, pointing dramatically to himself, he added, "I too have sinned."

In the pause that followed, one of the residents leaned forward in her wheelchair and shouted, "What did you do, Pastor? What did you do?"

—John R. Pearson
Pleasantville, N. Y.

The Rewards of Prayer

For years now my favorite hobby has been position target shooting with a small-bore, 22-caliber rifle. I've been a member of several teams and enjoy competition.

During a tournament in Waukesha, Wis., I came off the line after firing a round from the kneeling position. A member of the other team, who knew I was a pastor, asked me how I had done.

"I think I scored a hundred," I answered.

"That's really not fair, you know," he said.

"What do you mean, it's not fair?" I inquired. "I work awfully hard at this."

His answer: "It's not fair, Pastor, because you've had so much practice on your knees!"

—The Rev. Alvin Pinke
Bakersfield, Calif.

Thus Says the Pastor

Hoping to keep small hands off an elaborate stereo set in our social rooms, the pastor made a large sign. "This is the eleventh commandment," it read. "Thou shalt not touch the stereo system. Signed, The Pastor."

A few weeks later, someone wrote this on the bottom of the sign: "Pastor, thou shalt not make additional commandments. Signed, The Lord."

—Glenda Sturtevant
Friedens, Pa.

Sign Up in Secret

I'm a pastor who teaches a weekly adult inquirers' class for anyone who wants to know what our church teaches and practices. Imagine my surprise when a local columnist made this announcement: "The adulterers' class will be held at 7:30 p.m."

—The Rev. L. Wayne Myers
Merritt Island, Fla.

On Second Thought . . .

During the early weeks of his seminary internship, a friend of mine was asked to conduct the liturgical portion of the Sunday service. The pastor carefully instructed him and rehearsed the liturgy with him in the "new," red *Service Book and Hymnal.* On the Saturday before his debut, my friend spent several hours in the empty sanctuary practicing his part until he was confident he had mastered it.

Sunday morning came. As he progressed through the liturgy, he suddenly discovered that he had lost his place in the service book. Sensing panic but thinking quickly, he turned to the waiting congregation with the invitation "Let us pray." Everyone bowed in devout anticipation.

Then the young intern turned back to the altar, glanced at the service book, and, just as suddenly, found the proper place. Without wasting another moment, he swung back to face the congregation and issued another invitation: "Let us not pray."

—The Rev. Frank E. Wilcox
Fullerton, Calif.

Some Eulogy, Pastor

I don't recall who told me this one, but he said it really happened. I believe him.

Anyway, there was this Norwegian Lutheran pastor, older than most of us, who was much more comfortable with the "mother tongue" than with English. But he was shepherding an American congregation and hence had to speak English most of the time.

Once, during a funeral, he was preaching a passionate sermon. Among other things, he wanted to communicate that, after death, a person's spirit leaves his or her body.

Pointing to the departed, who was lying in an open casket, the pastor offered this helpful metaphor: "Vhat ve have here is yost the shell. The nut is gone."

—David L. C. Anderson
Anoka, Minn.

Not Quite Perfect

An Air Force chaplain, a Southern Baptist, spent several evenings with our group of young missionaries in Darjeeling, northeast India. He and some of his men

..."YOST THE SHELL.
THE NUT IS GONE."
LANCE BOWEN

were on leave from one of the American airfields in Bengal from which tons of supplies had been flown over "the Hump" (Himalayas) into China during World War II.

One evening when we were exchanging stories, he recounted memories of the first wedding he had performed in his first parish. Our chaplain friend knew the wedding would be the outstanding event of the social season in that small southern Oklahoma town. It would bind in matrimony the son of the local physician and the daughter of the local banker. So to avoid any fumbling or stumbling during the service, he practiced several hours each day for at least two weeks. The wedding rehearsal was a model of smooth pastoral performance.

The day of the wedding came—a sultry, southern Saturday. In the packed church the air was heavy with the scent of flowers. "The service moved along effortlessly," our chaplain friend recalled. "Then I came to the climactic moment. With finality in my voice, I solemnly intoned, 'and now I pronounce you male and female.' "

—The Rev. Frank E. Wilcox
Fullerton, Calif.

Best Wishes from John

A pastor friend of mine says he'll never forget it. After performing the wedding, he mingled with guests at the reception. The best man was acting as emcee, introducing friends of the newlyweds and making appropriate remarks.

One of those remarks was interrupted by a Western Union delivery boy. The best man opened the telegram and announced: "It's a Scripture reference for the bride and groom—'John 4:18.' That's all it says."

Now the reference was supposed to be **1** John 4:18: "There is no fear in love, but perfect love casteth out fear. . . ." But what does Western Union know about 1 John, John, or any other book in the Bible? So the telegram simply read "John 4:18."

One of the guests, New Testament in hand, turned to that verse and read this message for all to hear: "For thou hast had five husbands, and he whom thou now hast is not thy husband. . . ."

—F. Carlton Booth
Monrovia, Calif.

Token of Appreciation

Some years ago a minister friend of mine married a couple who didn't belong to his church. After the ceremony, the groom said, "Reverend, I don't have any money, but I do work for the gas company. So if you'll direct me to your cellar, I'll fix your meter so it'll never register again."

—Anne G. Rice
Zelienople, Pa.

Will the Real Jesus . . .

A tough five-year-old named Margaret came to our mission chapel in Sunderland, England, one Sunday and asked, "Where's Jesus?" Someone pointed to a painting of Christ on the wall.

"That ain't Jesus," huffed Margaret. "It's only a

pitcher!" Then she turned to her companion and said, "C'mon, Valerie. Jesus ain't in this place."

—The Rev. Arnold E. Kromphardt
Buffalo, N. Y.

You're Watering My Hat

Many years ago a Boston friend of mine went to one of the elite funeral homes in Brookline. On her way to the service, she purchased a new hat—an extremely showy, floral affair fashionable in those days.

At the home she realized the hat had to go—at least during the service. So she left it on a table in the foyer, safe for the moment, she thought.

Imagine her surprise several minutes later when she joined the others to view the departed's peaceful remains. Right in the center of the casket's unopened half was her hat—the most striking floral piece of all!

—F. Carlton Booth
Monrovia, Calif.

Performing a Funeral Circus

A funeral director called me and said, "I hear you're a chaplain in the Air Force."

"Well, I'm in the Reserve," I said.

"There's a lady whose husband just died, and she wants someone with a military background to perform the funeral because he was in the Air Force."

"OK," I said.

At the chapel everything was in order for the service—except for the widow, who wasn't there. We waited 20 minutes, then she popped in through a side door and started screaming, "O my beloved! O my beloved!" Before I knew what was happening, she jumped on top of the casket and sobbed, "What will I do now? I can't live without you!" On and on . . .

Recovering for a moment, I turned to the funeral director and said, "We've got to get her off the casket." We did—with no little difficulty. The rest of the service was a blur.

After the benediction, Old Pierre, the town's only photographer, came up to me and announced, "She wants me to take pictures." So he started flashing: the deceased, the widow and the deceased, the deceased and me, then all three of us.

At graveside there was a band that played before and after my part. A few more photos, and the ordeal was over. I thought . . .

A year later I got a call from the same funeral director. "Remember the service you did for that Air Force widow?" he asked.

"How could I forget?" I said.

"Well," said the director, "she married another guy, and he died too. Since you did such a fine job last time, she wants you again."

How I ended up in that chapel a second time, I'll never know. We went through the same routine: screaming, casket, photos, band. I should have known.

Another year passed, and the director called a third time. "Now she's died," he said, "and the family wants you."

How could I say no to family tradition?

Nothing bizarre happened this time until we got to the cemetery. There I was astounded to discover that the grave of one of her late husbands—they'd been buried side by side—was empty. He'd been moved a few

"NOW I LAY ME DOWN TO SLEEP..."
LANCE BOWEN

feet west, and, sure enough, we plopped her right down between them.

R.I.P!

—The Rev. Wally Klandrud
Phoenix, Ariz.

Hands Together, Eyes Closed

Because they are so familiar with the liturgy, pastors and laypersons at times may worship unthinkingly. Brains aren't always fully in gear on Sunday morning.

Not long ago a pastor told me about a colleague of his who was leading worshipers in the closing parts of the service. Turning toward the altar for the Lord's Prayer, he stretched out his arms and began, "Now I lay me down to sleep. . . ."

—David L. C. Anderson
Anoka, Minn.

Good News, Bad News

I had an intern in San Bernardino, Calif., who was especially good in the pulpit. One Sunday I sent him to preach at a neighboring congregation.

After the service the people filed out the door, expressing their enthusiasm for his preaching. One old gent, though, grabbed my intern's hand and said, "Reverend, that was a good sermon. You've got a long way to go."

—The Rev. Les Hoffmann
Phoenix, Ariz.

Dehydrated Baptism

It was embarrassing! Parents, sponsors, and child were up front. I signaled to an acolyte, who removed the lid from the baptismal font. Horrors! There wasn't a drop of water in the thing. But we went through with it anyway, fooling most of the congregation.

After the service the child's father cornered me in the narthex. "Well, Pastor," he boomed, "now that we've had the dry run, shouldn't we do it for real?"

—The Rev. Les Hoffmann
Phoenix, Ariz.

Hint, Hint!

In my first parish I was determined to get to know the members as quickly as possible. So during my debut as worship leader and preacher, I invited my parishioners to an open parsonage. "Please be there with your presence," I said sincerely.

A choir member seated near the pulpit almost burst out laughing. I was puzzled—but only for a moment. We were in the middle of Advent!

—The Rev. Conrad Lund
Issaquah, Wash.

And the Lord Said, "Uffda!"

The executive council of one of the Lutheran church bodies was in session. On the agenda: discussion of the need to discontinue using Swedish for worship services and shift entirely to English.

One pastor refused to yield. "It's our responsibility to minister to Swedes in their native tongue," he declared.

A council member looked him in the eye and asked, "Do you believe the Lord understands English?"

Returning stare for stare, the pastor replied, "He understands it, but he doesn't like it!"

—The Rev. Kenneth L. Engstrom
Miller, S. Dak.

Tickled to Death

While traveling to India for the first time, I was blessed with the company and counsel of a veteran missionary to South Africa. He had served among the Zulu people for 10 years and, after an absence of some time, was returnng to the work he loved.

Upon disembarking at Cape Town, he and I boarded a train for Durban, where I was able to catch a ship sailing eastward to Bombay. Enroute to Durban we stopped twice to visit missionary and Christian Zulu friends of his. At the Zulu Bible Institute in Pietermaritzburg, he was reminded of the first time he had preached to the tribespeople. So he told me about it.

Assisted by a skilled translator, my friend—unsure of his Zulu at the time—addressed a large youth gathering. One of his illustrations involved a man who was thrilled about an answer to prayer. Said my friend: "He was simply tickled to death." The Zulu interpreter looked puzzled, asked him to repeat the phrase, thought for a moment, and then rapidly spoke a sentence in Zulu.

After the meeting, veteran missionaries asked the young preacher if he knew how the interpreter had

HAVE YOU HUGGED YOUR RIFLE TODAY?
LANCE BOWEN

translated "He was simply tickled to death." My friend shook his head. "Well," said one of them, smiling broadly, "in Zulu it came out something like this: 'He itched and he itched and then he died!' "

—The Rev. Frank E. Wilcox
Fullerton, Calif.

Saved by Incompetence

A man in Ohio burst into church one Sunday morning, gun in hand. He ran up the center aisle, trained his weapon on the pastor, and shouted, "I'm going to kill myself, and then I'll kill you!"

In the hush that followed, the pastor spoke boldly: "OK, friend. If you want to do it that way, it's fine with me."

The gunman looked puzzled for a moment, then dropped his weapon. "Ah, shucks!" he said. "I can't do anything right!"

—The Rev. Wally Klandrud
Phoenix, Ariz.

Bon Voyage, Pastor

During the early years of my ministry, I was called to a congregation that had no definite policy on the pastor's vacation. Some members thought one Sunday; others, two. Each year I had to negotiate.

Finally one day, before a congregational meeting, I spoke with the chairman and suggested we put something "permanent" into the minutes about my vacation. He agreed.

During the meeting he made a little speech. Then, confident he had been persuasive, he called for the vote: "All those in favor of giving our pastor a permanent vacation, say aye."

—The Rev. Walter Schedler
Campbell, Calif.

Miserable Members

A woman asked her pastor for the birth record of her sister. The church files were searched, but to no avail.

Several days later the pastor approached her and asked, "Has your family always been connected with this congregation?" The woman's reply: "Why, sure. We've been afflicted with this church all our lives."

—The Rev. Kenneth L. Engstrom
Miller, S. Dak.

Feminist Baptism

I do pretty well with pronouns. Take the baptismal service, for example. You've got *him, her,* and sometimes *them.*

The service book I use starts with the masculine singular and includes feminine singular and plural pronouns in italics. You have to make changes when you're baptizing a baby girl or more than one infant.

Anyway, I baptized a baby girl during summer 1980 and handled the pronouns just fine—until the "charging questions" for the parents and sponsors. By that time I was geared up for the changes. So I asked them, "Do you renounce the devil and all her works and all her ways?"

—Chaplain John K. Stake
Selfridge Air National Guard Base, Mich.

Ladder-Day Saint

I'm a pastor who recently was helping a group of parishioners paint the sanctuary walls. We were using rollers. Suddenly, the ladder I was standing on slipped. I wasn't hurt, but the sliding ladder tore a hole in the carpet.

Quipped one of the volunteers who had witnessed the incident, "The holy roller has become a holy tearer."

—The Rev. Lloyd R. Hanson
Carmichael, Calif.

Preacher Praises Prisoners

A pastor in our community was asked to preach to the inmates of a county prison. Pleased by the invitation, he began by blurting out an enthusiastic "I'm glad to see so many here!"

—Conrad Lobel
Paxtang, Pa.

Asnooze in the Pews

Soon after I was installed as pastor of my congregation, a parishioner came to me wondering about the church's plans for *Lutheran Book of Worship.* "Are we going to start using that new Lutheran lethargy?" he asked.

—The Rev. Daniel M. Powell
Hilliard, Ohio

Tricks of the Trade

I was talking on the telephone in my office one day when my wife and two-year-old daughter came to church. They decided to wait in the sanctuary.

Approaching the altar rail, my wife said to Bethany, "Let's talk to God." While they were kneeling, Bethany slipped through the rail and went directly to the altar. Returning to my wife, who was still kneeling, she pretended to hand her something, saying, "Here's the bread." Then back to the altar, return, and "Here's the wine."

My wife was charmed until Bethany went back to the altar a third time and grabbed an offering plate. Turning around and shoving it in her mother's face, she said bluntly, "I need a dollar."

Clever preacher's kid!

—The Rev. Mark Huggenvik
Newbury Park, Calif.

A Marriage Made in Heaven

He had me worried. The groom went through rehearsal motions like a nervous robot. His bride was a model of composure.

She was calm the day of the wedding too. But her

husband-to-be stood up front stiffly, eyes glazed. He had me worried.

Time for the vows. I fixed what I hoped was a reassuring gaze on the groom (was he looking at me?) and said, "Repeat after me: 'I, Donald, in the presence of God and these witnesses . . .' "

There wasn't a sign in the groom's unblinking eyes that he had heard. I was about to try again when he droned, "I, God, in the presence of Donald and these witnesses . . ."

The guests tried—unsuccessfully—to stifle their laughter. I decided this was no time for corrections and continued on to the blessed relief of the benediction.

Six months later I received a Christmas card from the newlyweds. Their greeting began: "We're sure you remember us and our wedding, Pastor. It was the first time you ever married God!"

—The Rev. Edward Wessling
Denver, Colo.

Of Customs and Customers

When my wife and I first came as missionaries to Paranavai, a town in Brazil's interior, we had a free morning for sight-seeing. Spying a row of horse-drawn carts—each with a driver and room for two riders—we thought, What better way to see the town! So we hired a cart.

Up and down the streets we went, until we noticed a small Presbyterian church. I asked the driver to stop, went to the door, and knocked. The pastor answered. I introduced myself as the new Lutheran minister from America. He appeared pleased.

Then I pointed to my wife, who is very blond,

sitting in the horse-drawn cart. All of a sudden a surprised and shocked look came over his face. Abruptly, he excused himself. I was left standing there, mystified, with nothing to do but hop back in the cart. We continued our ride.

The reason for my Presbyterian colleague's behavior became embarrassingly clear several weeks later. Someone told us that those horse-drawn carts are used exclusively for transporting customers to the prostitution zone at the edge of Paranavai and to bring the girls to town. To make matters worse, the only women around as blond as my wife were "ladies of the night."

So we had spent our first morning masquerading all over town and at the Presbyterian church as prostitute and customer. What a way to start a ministry!

—The Rev. Jack C. Aamot
Bloomington, Minn.

Sunday Morning Show Stopper

While visiting at First Assembly Congregation in Eugene, Oreg., I noticed a lively youngster in the front row. He must have been about four years old.

He certainly was active, and his antics entertained the whole congregation during the hymns and the pastoral prayer. Seated several rows back, his mother tried repeatedly to get his attention. She failed.

Finally, just before the sermon, she walked briskly forward, grabbed her son by the shoulder, and began marching him down the aisle.

With each step he would drag his heels and yell, "No, Momma, no!" The battle drew every eye.

Then, a few feet from the narthex doors, the

LANCE

youngster apparently had a vision of his soon-to-be-realized fate. Just before disappearing, he cried out with great urgency: "Oh, my goodness! Somebody pray!"

It was a hard act for the poor minister to follow.

—Bonney Stuart
Washtucna, Wash.

A Time for Medication

A woman who has been a shut-in member of my congregation came to church recently. After the service she shook my hand and exclaimed, "I had to take two pain pills in order to come and listen to you preach."

—The Rev. George Schuette
Auburn, Ind.

A Higher Calling

When asked by a member of the congregation whether he wanted to be a preacher like his father, my five-year-old grandson replied, "I'd rather be God."

—Mrs. Ken P. Doyle Jr.
Granite Quarry, N. C.

That's Ministry!

I'm a pastor. One day, wearing my clerics, I visited my wife in the hospital following the birth of our third child. Before leaving I gave her an affectionate kiss.

After I had gone, my wife's hospital roommate

turned to her and exclaimed, "My, your minister is friendly!"

—The Rev. Larry A. McConnell
Spring Grove, Pa.

You're Swell, But . . .

It was a touching, tender moment. After exchanging vows, the couple continued to face each other, hands clasped. A chord, then the groom sang to his bride with great feeling, "I'd rather have Jesus. . . ."

—Dr. Donald M. Williams
La Jolla, Calif.

What Funny Thing Happened to You?

Do you have an original documented anecdote of your own that you would like to share with the readers of a sequel to this book? If so, mail it to

A FUNNY THING
Box 833
Anoka, MN 55418

All submissions will be acknowledged, and, if published, will be remunerated with a copy of the book in which they appear.

Remember—these must be anecdotes that you (or a named friend) experienced.

Now—let's hear it from you!